LONE LEAF DANCING

Photos and Poems
by
Dwayne Cole

Beautiful leaves.
How full of color and light!
Grandchildren's smiles

Table of Contents

Tree leaves teach
Life's ever changing cycles
Dance of nature

Preface

Live each season as it passes;
breathe the air, drink the drink,
taste the fruit, and resign yourself
to the influence of the earth.
—Henry David Thoreau

Henry David Thoreau,
sought the beauty of little things in daily life.
Thoreau went to Walden Pond seeking solitude
of self reflection—To live the life he dreamed.
Close inspection of the little things
enabled him to see with new eyes.
Nature invited him to take
an insect's view of the smallest leaf.
It was not just what Thoreau looked at that mattered;
it was what he saw—His inner self with new perspective:
confidence to live the life he imagined.

Photos are silent poems
Poems are photos that speak
Look, listen, and write—

This book featuring nature photographs

of Alaska's luminous beauty and poems of trees and leaves

reveals how our lives change with the passing seasons,

especially the coming of winter when leaves fall to the ground

to be covered with a blanket of purity.

The poems illustrate the delicate balance between life and death, helping us navigate the passage of time and loss of loved ones. Fall leaves teach us how to let go, but also how to dance anew after times of tragedy. Birch trees are the first to bud in cold climates like Alaska.

Robert Frost's birches bent from boys swinging from them.

In Alaska, birch trees bend from heavy accumulation of snow.

Sitting on my deck in Anchorage and seeing the birches bend,

brings back memories of growing up on a farm—

I loved climbing and swinging from trees. I still do.

Even though, as an 82 year old,

it is more contemplating climbing,

as I hug and talk to them.

Meditation
Sitting quietly viewing trees
Leaf mindfulness

When I climb trees
The whole world is a tree
I am a tree

Walking, I wonder,
am I a tall spruce tree
or a leaf trembling?

The tree is my mother
Nurturing me at her breast
Trees give me life

Leaves sing lullabies
Speak tender loving words
I listen with care

In a mobile world
Leaves teach mystical union
Call us back to our roots

Contemplating trees
Nurtures poetic mindfulness
Nature's mind

Trembling leaves
Mother Nature's beating heart
Breath of joy

Fresh air
Flows through world
Renewing life

Introduction

The clearest way into the universe is through a forest.
                                                    —John Muir

For thousands of years humans have variously worshipped

trees, made use of them, admired them, and often carelessly

destroyed them. Poets from Homer, Virgil, Wordsworth,

Whitman, Thoreau, and modern day poets have spoken of tree

magic. The results include some of our most beloved poems,

like Robert Frost's "Birches" that ends with the line—

"One could do worse than be a swinger of birches."

Each poet of the past is in me, as I write. I seek to add a union of

science and the humanities to express the transformative

spirit of poetry. Nature is a breathing sensitive reality that

welcomes us with story and song into one symphony with each

entity singing its unique notes. We all mutually belong in the co-

evolving world. These tree and leaf poems represent the different

growth stages of our relational lives, moving us to a

new adventurous aliveness, a new feeling

of wonder among all things.

Underlying these poems is an environmental concern,

expressed as a poetic ecology. This ecological concern is

essential if we want to have clean air to breathe and survive on

planet earth. According to E. O. Wilson, at least 976 tree

species out of 100,000 known to science worldwide are in

difficulty and facing extinction (See, Wilson, The Future of Life).

Those who have lived a long life, as I have, have seen many

friends and family members drop as leaves from the tree of life.

During the last two years of writing this book

I lost my oldest sister and an older brother.

In these times of grief, one feels like the lone leaf of fall.

Fall leaves teach us how to let go.

With each loss of family and friends,
I feel the growing need to grasp
and give shape to the meaning of life.

Each day I find myself opening to a new life
that is wide and timeless.
Much like a large silver birch tree with deep roots
and limbs reaching toward heaven.

In a world so transient and prone to self-destruction,

I offer these photos and poems—

As inspiration and encouragement.

Leaves become more radiant as they grow old—

Shine as light so colorful and bold!

Each leaf has worth.

Each has the power to amaze.

Leaves become beautiful
as they grow old. Shine as light—
Colorful and bold!

Value of Colorful Trees and Leaves

Evolutionary biologists recognize the importance of trees.

Trees provided hunters wide views of grazing animals,

as well as any dangerous enemies— animals and humans.

Even today when walking in Alaska, I always have a tree

in mind close by to climb from brown bears and to dodge

behind if a moose comes too close.

There is also healing values in noticing and observing flowers

and colorful leaves strewn along the path. The tundra of Alaska

has a rich and colorful variety of undergrowth, both plants and

small animals like the arctic ground squirrel.

(Arctic ground squirrel in Denali National Park, Alaska)

Nature really is our mother, giving us life at every moment.

We cannot survive without her. Nature is magical.

Creative artists, writers, and poets have recognized the

importance of trees and leaves. In Celtic mythology, birch

trees are given the name, "Lady of the Woods."

Trees reaching for sun

Leaves drifting down like butterflies

Birds searching for food

This little haiku provides a snapshot of Mother Nature's

relational nurturing ways as the Lady of the Woods. Golden leaves,

compelling beauty, the burst of flame—Quivering life

forces. Creative poems grow like new leaves budding and

flowering with luminous beauty.

Spring Season

Shown spring flowers
Red, yellow, purple delights
grandchild opens mouth
Become a child to enter
Glory of heaven's ways

Worm Moon Tree Buds

Take time to gaze at the March

full moon, often called the Worm Moon.

Passing the torch, the setting sun

kisses the rising moon.

The yawning earth blushes pink.

Ground is thawing and worms wiggle.

New buds are forming on tree limbs.

The world is so very beautiful

my soul is bursting at the seams.

New adventures are waiting!

Spring sun is sinking
Passing torch to rising moon
As wiggling worms knew

Spring Season Haiku

Winter's snowy weeks
have packed up and gone home
It's spring breakup time

All day sunlight near
Mountains singing joyful songs
Tree buds are popping

Mating songs are sung
Unfrozen frogs of Potter's Marsh
Croaking in rhythm

Bull moose are bugling
Tree buds bursting like popcorn
Shiny green leaves

Hearing spring music
I salute, dance, and sing
my songs of praise

Moon bride is coming
to caress with tender beams
of love and light

All day sun coming
Mountains singing joyful songs
Tree buds are popping

Hearing spring music
I stand in salute and sing
My songs of praise

After long wait in dark
New tender life bursts forth
Light returns again

Life is leaf on tree

Unfolds from a bud in spring

Water color scenes

It grows in the warm sun of summer

and sings of earth and sky.

Joining with other leaves

it does its best work.

Giving the very air we breathe,

beauty and grace to inspire.

Makes us whole.

Summer Season

Nature's vibrant green leaves
Mysterious Oneness
Joyful peacefulness

Is summer here indeed?

The green leaves quivering, yes!

Grebes float like leaves.

Awe and wonder in the presence of mystery

is the source of poetry.

Gazing at these scenes

framed by quivering green leaves,

I am wrapped in awe and wonder.

I become a leaf.

Understand earth better.

Nature is sublime.

Fall Season

Nature's beauty

has power to consecrate—

Purity of heart.

In its branches, trees

make room for the birds

to come and join

in its chorus of praise.

The leaves become a mosaic of colors

in the frost of fall.

Seeking to make their mark, they dance

in wonder of snow capped peaks all around.

Chugach beaming

The whole sky a rainbow

Leaves trembling

Chugach Mountain Peaks

As the sun went down on Chugach

they turned into peppermint candy mountains.

The leaves turned into lemon gum drops

on big rock candy mountain.

The sky and mountains kiss ever so shy.

Clouds wink, blushing pink.

Birds sing praise.

Chugach beautiful

After evening shower

Yellow peppers

Fall leaves glowing.

Lips moist with Muses' nectar.

Be still and listen!

The mornings shine harmony.

The evenings peaceful sleep.

Nature's beauty

has power to consecrate—

Purity of heart.

Alaska gold rush
Leaves falling from birch trees
Coins for memory bank

To change into a spruce tree
Grow for many years not hurting anyone
Give shelter to birds in storms

Inspire with golden needles
Glowing in the evening sun
Moses' burning bush
Glory came down
dancing and swirling around

Bow in worship

Golden birch leaves
Heaven's glory is shining
Angels thinking light

Golden birch singing
Reaching for Robin egg skies
Inspire lofty thoughts

Lifts the human spirit
Ennobles the human soul
Nature shines for all

Silver birch trees
Minting golden coins
Climb and become

Autumn minting gold,
for memory bank account.
Nature's rich gifts!

Autumn leaves golden
For memory bank account
Snow skis down mountain

Larch spruce needles
Swaying to and fro in rhythm
Stitching warm blankets

In Autumn breeze
Birch leaves sing joyful tune
Geese are flying

Golden birch leaves
Sunshine smiles of grandchildren
Life's precious gifts

To sit in quietness
With golden leaves dancing jig
Balm for hurting heart

The Lady of the Woods
Symbol of new beginnings
magical healing

Quiet please.
Leaves softly singing—
Art show in progress!

D. Cole

Become like a tree
Climb and touch Luna's robe
Mighty spruce magic

Want to be Sitka Spruce
Needles stitching life giving shelter
Haven for nesting birds

Sometimes I wish
To be a silver birch tree
Give shelter to birds
Grow without hurting anyone
Inspire all with golden leaves

Ode to Magic of Autumn Days

Elves spin and dance

Snow is coming down mountain

Bow often and give thanks

Mother Nature sings

Lifting songs of joyful praise

Alleluia! Alleluia!

All creation lifts the tune

Golden leaves fly up again!

Look warblers are back!

Catch a falling leaf.

Yellow tundra cottonwood leaf.

It's a butterfly!

I want to believe,
be dazzled by mystery!
Look, golden leaves!

White paper birch bark.
Sketch pad for glowing red leaves.
Quiet, Nature's art show!

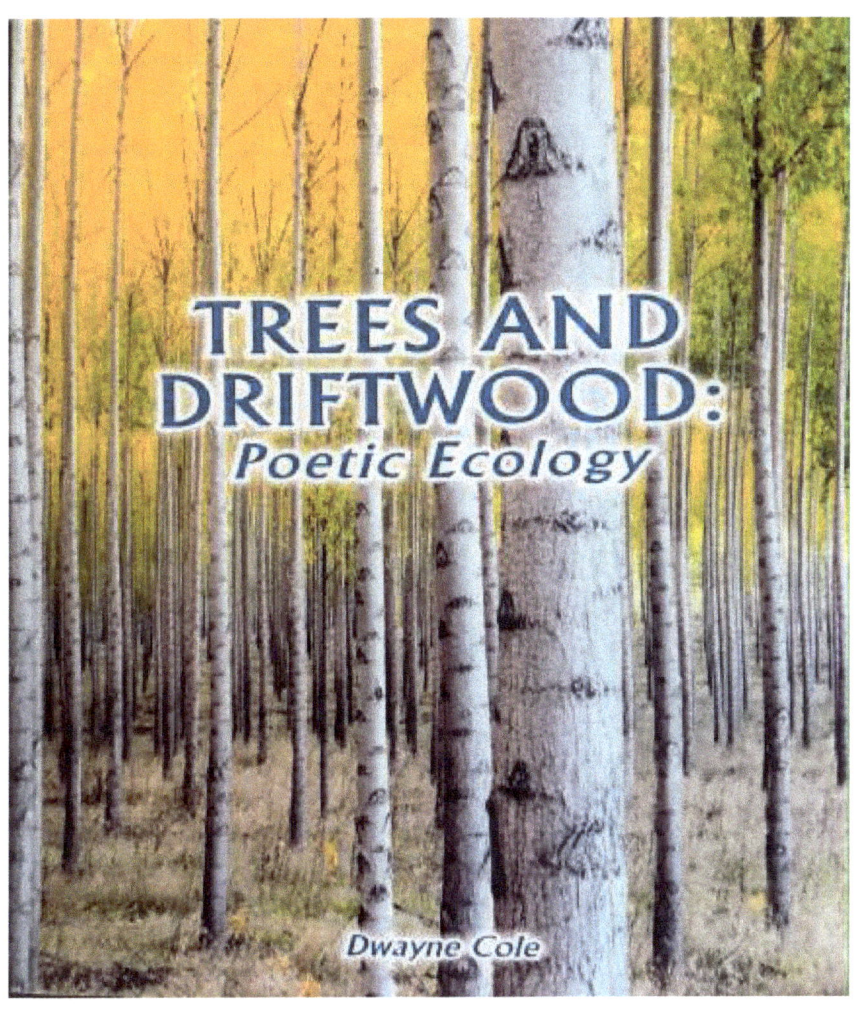

Silver birch trees
Driftwood on sandy beaches
Poetic ecology

(See my book, TREES AND DRIFTWOOD on Amazon, Todd
Communications, and Barnes&Nobles on line)

Leaves don't despair

Daily absorb nature's gifts

Heaven comes down

Silver Birch Trees

Hands full
of blessings

Reaching into
blue skies

Minting gold coins
Richness flowing for all

Gather astonishment
Feel the joy

Store treasures
in your memory bank

Happy light
for dark winter days

Alaska's gold rush

Tundra leaves singing

Golden coins falling

Tundra is painted

Sun is climbing the mountains

Harvest moon waiting

Shovel turning mulch
Breathe deeply the earth scent
The breath of Gaia

I love to climb trees
Get away for awhile
Sit quietly in the heavens
Till my heart is filled with love

Climb high touch Aeolus,
the Greek God of wind
Hear aeolian music
In trembling leaves

Watch the cirrus clouds
Swim by
Big as whales
In the blue sea sky

Climbing to the tip top
Touch the silver robe of Luna
The Roman goddess of the moon
Feel soul-quakes

Soak up the sun's warm rays
Capture the magic of our days
Oh, the wonder
Of climbing birch trees

(Photos of common redpolls from my deck in Anchorage, Alaska)

Redpoll blossoms
Falling like Autumn leaves
They fly up again

Falling Leaves

Snow is falling on mountains.
Prophesying colder days.

Termination dust.
Ending fall and beginning winter.

Golden birch leaves have fallen.
Cottonwood leaves turning yellow.

Still lots of gold coins to store
in memory bank for winter darkness.

Larch spruce needles swaying to and fro
stitching warm blankets.

To cover ground
soon to be freezing from snow.

Each falling leaf.
Each golden needle.

Softly falling.
Inviting lutes to play with them.

Toy soldiers
to march with them.

Bringing dreams for my pillow
on moonless midnights.

In the darkness,
I see the light.

that turns the leaves
into whispers of love.

Bringing new visions
of hope to me.

Then come the cold winds of winter
etching broken brown and gray scenes.

Life becomes
a swirling cycle of dark nights and cloudy days.

Picking up the fallen leaves
and holding them in your hands,

you can smell
the end-of-summer sadness.

They wave to their friends nearby,
holding infinity in their ribbed cages.

They cling to hope!

Then the harsh storms
send them scattered to the ground below,

as though they were
leaping out of their closed coffins,
all mummy brown
and dance on the ground.

Like children we watch
this parade of leaves
as if one day the stone
will roll away from our sepulchral door

and we will come out dancing
with the leaves that are twisting
and shouting where earthworms wiggle
and beetles hide their eggs.

Mother Nature's Art

Speaks to my heart

Gives me new eyes

for seeing

Beauty all around

In leaves on the ground

In every heart beat

Love is found

Walking in nature

Light shines on fallen leaves

I dance in wonder

Fall Leaves

Fall in Alaska

Sunshine leaves are falling

Grass turning yellow

Family of leaves

Gather on deck rail as one

For love's last touch

Winter Season

When all leaves are gone
Mother Nature makes diamonds
Sparkling snow leaves

Lone Leaf Dancing

A snowy morning

Lone leaf dancing in wonder

Tree limbs quivering

Lone Leaf Contemplative

I often sit as Autumn is waning
Contemplating one lone leaf

Shivering in cold
Gently swaying

Barely hanging on
Soon to fall

With nutrients drawn from the soil
Sunshine beaming down

The tree becomes a mother
Giving nourishment to the leaves

Linked by a stem it is easy to see
The leaf and tree are one

In similar ways
We are linked to Mother Nature

We are joined
To all things as one

Many as one
One as many

Perishing
Yet living Eternally

Dwayne Cole

Having no friends

        to enjoy the sunrises and sunsets—

               The leaf is lonely!

But held on.

As though it were glued to the tree limb.

It spoke briefly to his loved ones gone.

Am I the only one, all alone in the world?

Lone leaf falls to ground.

Two cottonwood leaves

caught and tenderly held

by spruce limbs. Rejoiced all summer

as raindrops glistened on each.

Glowed together in each rising sun.

Hard to let go of friends at sunset.

Winter snows will cover all

with a soft blanket of purity.

(When I viewed this photo, I could not believe how much

the leaf looked like a person climbing. Enlarge photo to see stem)

Lone leaf Climbing—

As I reach the mountain top
I ask, "May I sit and rest a spell?"
"Please do," said the mountain.
"But sit quietly, I have an art show going on."

Filled with wonder,
and transformed by the beauty,
the lone traveler is ready for a new sunrise—
On the other side.
Immortality! A present gift.
Eternity is now!

In winter when trees
have no singing leaves—
Nature forms snow leaves.

Winter solstice
COVID-19 variants raging
Sowing flower seeds

From bedroom window
Snow blanket covers everything
Grateful for sunshine

As darkness descends
Setting sun shines spotlight
Lift up your eyes

When all leaves are gone
Mother Nature makes diamonds
Sparkling snow leaves

Seasons come and go
Yet, we're fearful of dying
Snow leaves are falling

In falling of leaves,
the world is uncreated
No leaf is left.

But wait!

With serendipitous joy
the lonely leaf finds
that it is reunited
with its family and friends.

It dances in joy
with its old friends
as the gentle winds
blow to and fro.

The greatest joy comes
when the leaf learns
that every you is an I,
and every I is a you.

And each has worth.
Each has the power to amaze

When there is no leaf left
evolution re-creates one.

New Spring Season

Butterfly whispers.

Green leaves softly singing—

World wakes to beauty!

A society grows great when old men
plant trees in whose shade they know
they shall never sit. —Greek Proverb

New buds are forming

Unfolding from winter sleep

Blue skies smiling

Planting seedlings

Robins visiting looking for lodging

A place to sing

In every new spring

the trees burst into buds giving rise

to fresh growth.

New leaves dance with sweet music.

A new generation is born—

A resurrection!

New life blossoms with beauty like an oil painting.
The world is recreated in each new shining leaf.

You and I would not be here
without the leaves on the tree of life.

They take the carbon dioxide we breathe out,
mix it with the light from the sun.

Change it into the breath of life
we breathe in.

Living like a leaf on the tree that time built
is the mystery of mysteries!

Quiet please.

Leaves softly singing—

World wakes to beauty!

D. Cole.

Climb high in the birch tree.
Sit quietly.

Become
one of the limbs.

Listen to the music
of the trembling leaves.

Feel soul-quake.

Watch the cirrus clouds swim by.
Big as whales in the blue sea sky.

One can be transformed
by climbing birch trees!

D. Cole

Become like a tree
Climb and touch Luna's robe
Mighty spruce magic

O

Tip

of spruce

reaching for moon

affirming magic wand

sway gracefully in the wind

Stand strong in snow blizzards

Welcome birds for nesting season

Sing aeolian music of heavenly spheres

Put down deep roots receiving rich nutrients

While reaching for the alpenglow clouds

Oh for the patience to touch

the hem of Luna's robe

Sing aeolian songs

I wish to become

a spruce tree

Not hurting any one

Leaves in waterfall
Grace of luminosity
Look, gull feathers

Reverence for Trees and Leaves

Shimmering leaves
Ripples on Cheney lake
Grown from earth and sky

Conclusion

This book, *Lone Leaf Dancing,* has been growing in my heart and mind for several decades. Actually, growing up on the farm, trees were a daily experience of beauty and wonder.

These photos and poems of trees and leaves have been taken and written in my retirement in Alaska during the last decade. Alaska's trees and leaves, illumined by Alpenglow sunrises and sunsets, are incredibly beautiful.

Experiencing Alpenglow miracles, I was invited into a fire dance of wonder. I entered Tolkien's mythical world described in his book, The Lord of the Rings, where trees, Ents, walked and talked. Inspired, I wrote these haiku—

Ents, forest shepherds,
Slowly growing, nurturing
Patience, Ruling Ring

Ages of memory
Slow steady giving of life
Breath of fresh air

From deep root sprouts
To high blue bird egg skies
Giving us slow care

Silver birch trees
Hope is a tree with leaves
Golden leaves

How I love tree leaves
Haven for birds in snow storms
Nature's supreme gifts

Art is the tree of life. —William Blake

Trees are family
Leaves give breath and new life
Grow side by side

Trees fall from blight
Forest rise up in new light
Trees are family

Family leaves forever
Reaching for the morning light
Perishing yet eternal

I want to portray

golden silver birch leaves—

Poems that no one has heard!

Living like a leaf

Bursting forth on tree of life

Mystery of mysteries!

Life is like a leaf that time builds.

Unfolds from a bud in the spring—

The artist's watercolor scenes.

It grows in the life-giving sun of summer.

Sings of earth and sky.

In its branches it makes room

for birds to come and join

in its songs of praise.

as they grow old

Leaves become more radiant—

Shine as light so colorful!

I want to spend life

tending what grows and gives us

the air we breathe.

God, You are the tree of life.

Prophets, apostles, and saints

are fruit bearing branches.

Wisdom of ages

is stored in tree of life.

Waiting to bear fruit.

All are called to be coworkers.

I am a Lone Leaf Dancing.

Appendix A: Grandchildren, Our Leaf Poets

Your eyes look at us
Loving what can not be seen
Hope is beaming

Eager wakefulness
Green leaves shining forth brightly
Robins of spring

Our grandchildren
becoming tree poets
make us happy

Eternity
In trees and shining leaves
Heaven is now

We gaze into your eyes.
What does the future hold?
What will you see?

You gaze at us,
loving what we cannot see.
Spring leaves singing!

Dream dreams.
Dance in wonder.
Leaves growing beautiful!

(See tree poems by Cole and Clara at age 11 and 12 in my book,
TREES AND DRIFTWOOD: Poetic Ecology)

Appendix B: More Lone Leaf Haiku

What's the use of a fine house if you do not have a tolerable planet to put it on? —Henry David Thoreau

Leaf mind,

Spirit of eternity—

Be kind to trees.

Many of the poems in this book are written in haiku format.

Haiku is often the first poetry taught to children. It began in thirteenth century Japan as the opening phrase of renga, a long oral poem. The short haiku broke away from renga in the sixteenth century. Haiku, using provocative, colorful images, focuses on a brief moment in time when we slow down and see nature scenes like an alpenglow sunrise or sunset transforming the whole sky, mountains and trees. Haiku has a deep appreciation of nature. Having evolved in nature and interconnected with all things, we as humans are closely related to mountains, streams, and wildlife in empathy. Thus, haiku is especially suited to speak of trees and colorful leaves dancing.

Haiku often ends with a surprising sense of enlightenment. It is in this aha moment that the leaves sing our heart awake, revealing truths from unknown realms. We see with new eyes and hear with new ears, dancing into new adventures. We may not know where we are going, but we feel a new way has been opened.

The format of haiku is three lines, with the first and third lines each having 5 syllables, and the second line having 7 syllables. However, the emphasis is on three lines with an economy of words, not a total of 17 syllables. The syllable count may vary in each line—brevity that avoids over use of metaphors and simile is key. Sensory experience is the goal. The poet, Mary Oliver, hugged lichen covered oak trees; and talked with them. Hugging and climbing long after people advised her she was too old to climb.

When I climb trees
The whole world is a tree
I am a tree

The tree is my mother
Nurturing me at her breast
I grow in tenderness.

Autumn leaves whisper
The leaves speak words
I speak words back

In a mobile society,
always on the move,
trees teach mystical union.

Call us back to roots
Intertwined with each other
We are all one

I practice tree meditation
Sitting quietly and viewing trees
Leaf mindfulness

Autumnal leaves
Reminder of colorful summer days
Alpenglow warmth

Remembering kin
Fallen leaves from family tree
Golden birch leaves

Bird bath
Floating red leaf
In the wooden bowl

Sparkling diamonds
Morning dew drops on leaves
Redpoll sipping

Simplicity
Water, fruit, vegetables
Basel leaf aroma

Late autumn leaves fall
Teaching us how to let go
Yet humans grieve

7.2 earthquake
Spruce limbs quivering
Reach out to me

After the earthquake
The leaves stopped shaking
Stars shined bright

Trembling leaves
Beating heart of nature
Breath of joy

Falling leaf farewell
Faith is letting go of grip
Gentle rain drops

Sitting on my deck
yellow leaves fall lazily.
Look, warblers are back!

Trees in first Garden
Adam and Eve gaze in awe
The beauty of leaves

Grace of wild nature
The beauty of trees time built
Golden leaves trembling

Tolkien trees walk
Ents speak words of wisdom
Golden birch library

Snow falling on leaves
Breathing purity with us
Linus' blanket

Autumn leaves
Spinning and flashing
Power of wind

Sunrise miracle
Each raindrop on a leaf
Silent prayer

Dancing music
Cottonwood leaves falling
Spirit wind

Redpoll blossoms fall
Blake's starry heaven unfolds
Grasp infinity in hand

Winter in Alaska
Trees without a single leaf
Nakedness of winter

Heaven's epiphany
Limbs reaching to embrace
Hug grandchildren

Harvest moon
Tree shadows fall on floor
Child reaching for limbs

Winter blizzard
Lone leaf falls on snow
Shadow the poem

Corona virus
Pandemic war on nerves
Leaves dropping fast

Leaves on trees
Reveal most clearly
Our life cycle

Birch trees bend with snow
Reaching down to caress me
Leaves twist and turn

Mother Nature's wand
Leaves bursting with beauty
A grandchild's bright smile

White beard shining
Under golden birch leaves
Dreamer dreaming

Plant trees in spring
Make a place for nesting birds
To sing summer awake

Humans must turn back
Hear shimmering leaves singing
Rediscover music

Golden birch leaves
Sunshine smile of grandchildren
Life's precious gifts

Golden birch leaves
Capture the setting sun rays
To shine with the moon

What happens to leaves
Red, yellow, and golden leaves
After they fall down

Leaves fall and lose light.
Is there still heaven's light?
A personal heaven?

Who made the trees,
taught them how to grow leaves?
Oh precious children?

I want to believe,
be dazzled by mystery!
Look, golden leaves!

Leaf within me knows
All other leaves are family
Wisdom of sages

Leaves in my hand
Trees in my eyes shining.
Fruit is ripening

Trees into leaves
Leaves into trees
I am tree and leaf

Trees to leaves
Leaves to tree always
Inspire awe in me

The tree of life
The mysterious life force
Trees filling with buds

The tree of life
Wind of spirit blowing leaves
Our breath song

Autumn leaves turning
Teach us how to age gracefully
Caring for each other

Winter solstice nears
Dark cold days and nights depress
Spruce trees stay green

Cold white morning
Leafless trees throwing snow balls
Winter's beauty

Golden birch leaves
Sunshine smile of grandchildren
Life's precious gifts

Golden birch leaves
Capture the setting sun rays
To shine with the moon

What happens to leaves
Red, yellow, and golden leaves
After they fall down

Leaves fall and lose light.
Is there still heaven's light?
A personal heaven?

Tree still has branches
Birds are still singing joyfully
Wildflowers still bloom

I want to believe,
be dazzled by mystery!
Look, golden leaves!

To sit in quietness
With golden leaves dancing jig
Balm for hurting heart

Like leaf on a tree
We live in a cosmic dance
Fire dance of wonder

Always becoming
Yet, eternally ceasing
Wrapped in beauty

In spring solstice
Light comes in shining leaves
Dark shadows recede

A mighty forest
is in one tiny acorn
Squirrel buries one

Life without love
A tree without blossoms
Prune the tree

Leaf reaches mountain top
Cast eyes upon eternal shores
Loved ones are waiting

Other Books by Dwayne Cole

Sometimes I wish
To be a silver birch tree
Give shelter to birds
Grow without hurting anyone
Inspire all with kindness

A Center that Holds: Adventures in Kindness
Alpenglow Miracles: Fire Dance of Wonder
A Prayer of Blessing: As You Go Remember This
A Relational Hermeneutic of Kindness
A Relational Trinity of Kindness
BEARS AND MOOSE OF ALASKA: Nature Poetry
Clouds of Inspiration
Down on the Farm in Georgia: A Poetic Memoir
Dragonfly Magic
Gentle Galilean Glories: The Tender Teachings of Jesus
God and Evil: An Ode to Kindness
Jesus' Transforming Beatitudes: Selected Sermons from Year A
Jesus' Transforming Love: Selected Sermons from Year B
Jesus' Transforming Gentle Teachings: Selected Sermons from Year C
Kindness Is Every Step: Photos and Poems
Poems Inspired by Process Philosophy
Poet of the Universe: A Vision of Beauty and Goodness.
The Apostles' Creed: A Living Creed for the Living Church
The Book of Revelation: Jesus' Kindness Transforms Suffering
The Serenity Prayer: A Pathway to Peace and Happiness
The Story of the Bible: Authority, Inspiration, Canonization, and Translation
TREES AND DRIFTWOOD: Poetic Ecology
WINGS OF INSPIRATION

Parson's Porch Books

Lone Leaf Dancing
ISBN: Softcover 978-1-955581-68-4
Copyright © 2022 by Dwayne Cole

Parson's Porch Books is an imprint of Parson's Porch *&* Company (PP*&*C) in Cleveland, Tennessee. PP*&*C is an innovative organization which raises money by publishing books of noted authors, representing all genres. Its face and voice is **David Russell Tullock** (dtullock@parsonsporch.com).

Parson's Porch *&* Company *turns books into bread & milk* by sharing its profits with the poor.

www.parsonsporch.com